NAVEGADOR SERIES℠

Shine

Principles to elevate your dreams to a new level of freedom

DR. ANITZA SAN MIGUEL

NAVEGADOR SERIES℠

NAVEGADOR SERIES: Shine

© Copyright 2023, Dr. Anitza San Miguel.
All rights reserved.

No portion of this book may be reproduced by mechanical, photographic or electronic process, nor may it be stored in a retrieval system, transmitted in any form or otherwise be copied for public use or private use without written permission of the copyright owner.

It is sold with the understanding that the publisher and the individual author are not engaged in the rendering of psychological, legal, accounting or other professional advice. The content and views in each chapter are the sole expression and opinion of the author and not necessarily the views of Fig Factor Media, LLC.

Cover Design by Marco Alvarez
Layout by LDG Juan Manuel Serna Rosales

Printed in the United States of America

ISBN: 978-1-95998928-8
Library of Congress Control Number: 2023906900

Scripture quotations taken from The Holy Bible, New International Version®, NIV®. Copyright© 1973, 1978, 1984, 2011 by Biblica, Inc.®
Used by permission. All rights reserved worldwide.

I dedicate this book series to all my spiritual mentors who have guided me throughout my life. You are all my inspiration. I have learned from each of you that without God in my life and without seeking His guidance and direction, my life would not be the same. Thank you! It is because of God's grace that I am where I am. It is because of you and your continuous support and prayers that have lifted me in my darkest moments.

NAVEGADOR SERIES℠

TABLE OF CONTENTS

Acknowledgments 5

Introduction 6

    ACTION 8

    ELEVATE 10

    LIFT 12

    GIVE 14

    JOY 16

    GRATITUDE 18

    OBSERVE 20

    APPLY 22

    RESPOND 24

    SEARCH 26

    KNOCK 28

    LISTEN 30

    FREEDOM 32

About the Author 34

ACKNOWLEDGMENTS

A special thank you to my mentor and friend, Jacqueline Ruiz. Thank you for believing in me and seeing the *"magix"* within me. Thank you for helping me build my legacy.

Also, a special thank you to my husband, Juan M. Morales. Thank you for all of your support and encouragement as I navigate this journey of entrepreneurship.

Thank you to my daughter, Andrea I. Morales, for listening and understanding mommy. You are special to me and God.

INTRODUCTION

When God puts an idea in my mind and heart, I listen and I take action. This book series was born of my personal and spiritual growth journey. Since the day *"Navegador"* was born, I knew I was embarking on a journey where my vision wasn't clear. What I have learned in the process is that time will teach me the lessons that I need to know. Time has taught me to wait on the Lord. God has not shown me exactly what I will find on my journey, but has equipped me for the journey. I am qualified for the work He has called me to do. I don't have the whole vision, but He is my guide. He is the lighthouse that illuminates my path.

My purpose is that this book, as other books in the Navegador Series, will serve you to grow the passion and potential that is inside you, so you can shine your unique light. If I did it, so can you. Everything is possible if you trust, believe, and take action.

Other books in this series are Reignite and Grow.

Blessings!

NAVEGADOR SERIES^{SM}

NAVEGADOR SERIES℠

Action

ACTION

Therefore, with minds that are alert and fully sober, set your hope on the grace to be brought to you when Jesus Christ is revealed at his coming."

1 Peter 1:13

The day I started to take action, things started to change for me. The day that I let go of my fears and doubts, I had the courage to take the first step. It was then that I focused on my personal (and spiritual) growth and development. While you wait, prepare and take action.

NAVEGADOR SERIES℠

Elevate

> "He has declared that he will set you in praise, fame and honor high above all the nations he has made and that you will be a people holy to the Lord your God, as he promised." *Deuteronomy 26:19*

Elevate your thoughts to a new level. Elevate yourself in the richness that is within you. God has given you the resources. Use them! He will elevate you. Trust and believe in Him.

Lift

STRONG PEOPLE DON'T PUT OTHERS DOWN, THEY LIFT THEM UP.

"Therefore encourage one another and build each other up, just as in fact you are doing." *1 Thessalonians 5:11*

In your walk through life, lift others you encounter in your path. At times, I felt I needed to lift others. In the process, I found out that I was being lifted as well. I invite you to help someone today. You may change someone's life.

NAVEGADOR SERIES℠

Give

GIVE

"Each of you should give what you have decided in your heart to give, not reluctantly or under compulsion, for God loves a cheerful giver." *2 Corinthians 9:7*

Give with a joyful heart. When you give without expecting something in return, what you give will come back multiplied. I feel overjoyed every time I have the opportunity to give someone a helping hand or even a smile.

Joy

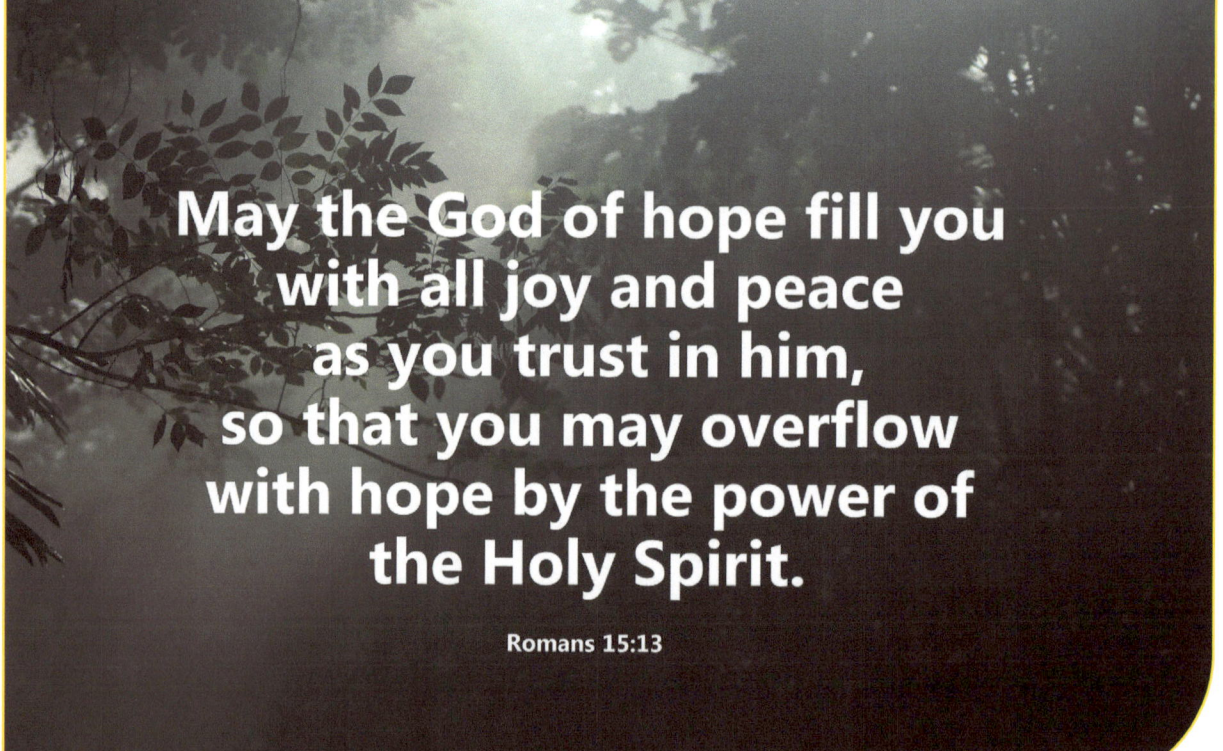

May the God of hope fill you with all joy and peace as you trust in him, so that you may overflow with hope by the power of the Holy Spirit.

Romans 15:13

Rejoice in the Lord always. I will say it again: Rejoice!"
Philippians 4:4

I am joyful. I rejoice in his promises. I rejoice in the time of need. I rejoice when everything is going smoothly. I rejoice in the middle of difficulty. Rejoice! As I soar to the next level, my heart is full of gratitude and expectation for what God will do. How are you feeling today?

NAVEGADOR SERIES℠

Gratitude

> Rejoice always, pray continually, give thanks in all circumstances; for this is God's will for you in Christ Jesus." 1 Thessalonians 5:16-18

Through the years, I have learned that it is impossible to be negative when you are grateful. Gratitude is the second highest frequency. Love is the first. In 2019, I developed the habit of writing what I am grateful for. It has been a game changer in my life! Being grateful for and in everything changed my perspective. What are you grateful for today?

Observe

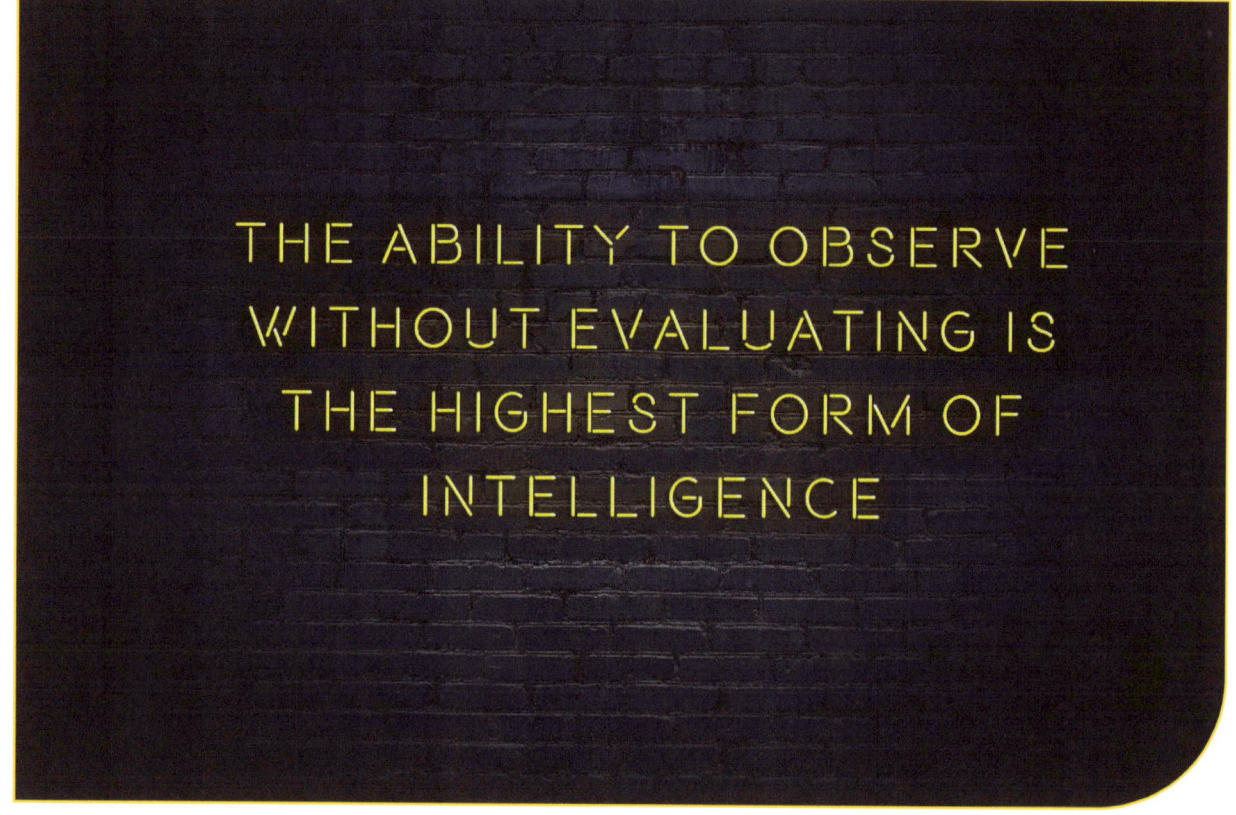

THE ABILITY TO OBSERVE WITHOUT EVALUATING IS THE HIGHEST FORM OF INTELLIGENCE

OBSERVE

Great are the works of the Lord; they are pondered by all who delight in them. Glorious and majestic are his deeds, and his righteousness endures forever." *Psalms 111:2-3*

Take time to observe your surroundings. We live on autopilot. We live "busy" lives and rarely is our busyness effective and productive. Today, stop to observe. Observe your surroundings, nature, and contemplate its beauty. When we pause to observe and reflect on how blessed we are, we start moving to a higher level of consciousness.

NAVEGADOR SERIES℠

Apply

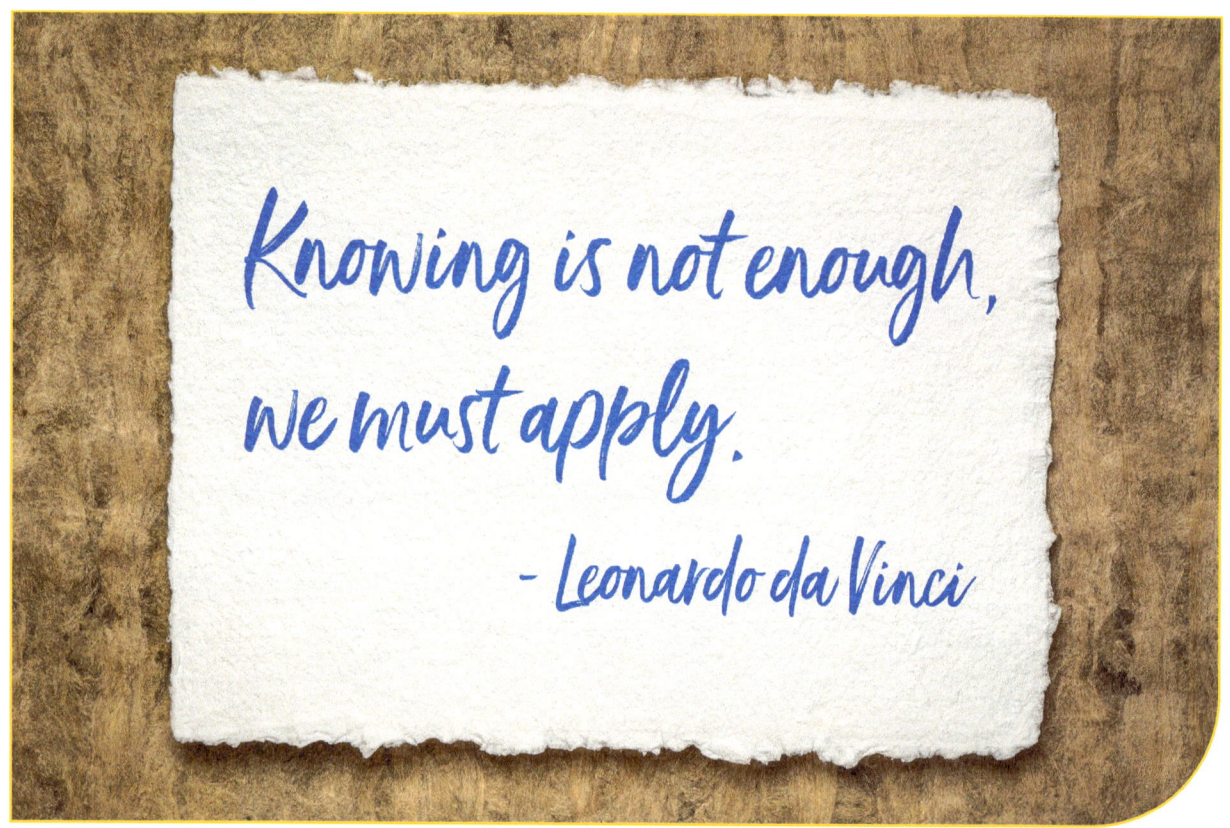

Knowing is not enough, we must apply.

— Leonardo da Vinci

APPLY

"Whatever you have learned or received or heard from me, or seen in me – put it into practice. And the God of peace will be with you." *Philippians 4:9*

I't's time for you to start applying what you have learned. I used to hoard information–yes, hoard. I felt I needed to know more to be ready. But I found out that I had to apply what I have learned to get better. Start applying all that knowledge that is in you.

NAVEGADOR SERIES℠

Respond

RESPOND

A person's wisdom yields patience; it is to one's glory to overlook an offense." *Proverbs 19:11*

Through my intentional growth journey, I have learned to respond and not react. It is so easy to react. When we react, we don't think. Every day ask God for wisdom and discernment so you can respond to the challenge and not react.

NAVEGADOR SERIES℠

Search

SEARCH

"You will seek me and find me when you seek me with all your heart." *Jeremiah 29:13*

Search for the Creator. Search for Him day and night. In the calmness of the early morning that's when I search for Him. If you seek, you will find.

Have you ever misplaced something valuable to you? I'm sure you have at some point. I have! In the process of finding what I misplaced, I learned to search calmly. When I search frantically for it, it takes more energy, and lots of stress. When I take the time to search for it calmly, I am able to find it without stressing about it.

NAVEGADOR SERIES℠

Knock

"Here I am! I stand at the door and knock. If anyone hears my voice and opens the door, I will come in and eat with that person, and they with me." *Revelation 3:20*

Have you felt a tug in your heart but you ignore it? That was me! God had been knocking on my door for a long time. I was too busy. I was too busy worrying about tomorrow. I was too busy living the life that others wanted me to live. When I decided to start moving in the direction I was called, things started to change for me. It is scary. It is unknown territory, but it's God's work. It is trusting, believing, and understanding that God is in control and that He will reveal his plan. Stop ignoring the knock. Open the door.

Listen

LISTEN for God's voice IN EVERYTHING you do

> So Eli told Samuel, "Go and lie down, and if he calls you, say, 'Speak, Lord, for your servant is listening.'"
> *1 Samuel 3:9a*

Listening is a skill that we all need to develop. We hear, but we rarely take the time to listen carefully. God may be speaking to you now through this book, but you are so distracted that you are unable to hear His voice. When God speaks to you, He does it in so many different ways. You have to be open to listen to His voice. Stop the distractions so you can hear His voice.

NAVEGADOR SERIES℠

Freedom

FREEDOM

It is for freedom that Christ has set us free. Stand firm, then, and do not let yourselves be burdened again by a yoke of slavery." *Galatians 5:1*

I am free. I always felt like a bird inside a cage. I cannot explain in words the pressure I felt on my chest. When I let myself be guided by God, who reignited my passion, I was free to be who I was created to be. I am a warrior. So are you!

ABOUT THE AUTHOR

Dr. Anitza San Miguel is wife, mom, scientist, educator, and transformational leadership coach. Her purpose is to help leaders reignite the potential and passion within them, so they can grow and shine their unique light, transform their mind, and unleash their potential to create their best version without limits.

Her passion for personal growth and development drives her to grow daily. She has more than twenty years of experience in research and education. She has served as a science professor and dean of science at institutions in Virginia and Florida, and currently serves as a dean leading a team in the Orlando, Florida area. She worked at the National Institutes of Health (NIH) and the United States Patent and Trademark Office (USPTO).

She is also the founder of ASM Mentors, creator of the podcast "Sacúdete y Toma Acción" translated in English as "Shake It Off and Take Action." Dr. San Miguel has

ABOUT THE AUTHOR

been showcased in numerous platforms in social media, and other events, including TV programs in Puerto Rico. She authored *Navegador*, a reflective journaling tool with reflection cards, and was featured as an insightful author in *Today's Inspired Latina Volume X* and *Today's Inspired Leader Volume IV* book series. She is also a sought-after speaker, mentor, and coach.

Dr. San Miguel firmly believes that everything is possible if you trust, believe, and take action. Her attitude, positive energy, and determination have led her to achieve her professional and personal goals.

When she's not working, you'll find her spending quality time with her husband and fourteen-year-old daughter, traveling, and journaling.

She is passionate about education that leads to the academic and professional success of leaders with the mission of discovering their best version without limits.

DR. ANITZA SAN MIGUEL
anitza@anitzasanmiguel.com
LinkedIn: /anitza-sanmiguel
Instagram: @anitza21
anitzasanmiguel.com

To view Dr. Anitza San Miguel's other books, please visit: anitzasanmiguel.com.

NAVEGADOR SERIES℠